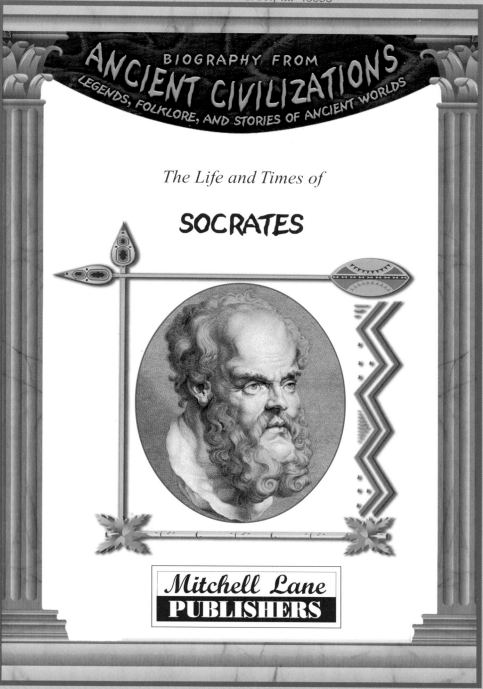

BIOGRAPHY FROM
ANCIENT CIVILIZATIONS
LEGENDS, FOLKLORE, AND STORIES OF ANCIENT WORLDS

The Life and Times of

SOCRATES

Mitchell Lane
PUBLISHERS

P.O. Box 196
Hockessin, Delaware 19707

BIOGRAPHY FROM
ANCIENT CIVILIZATIONS
LEGENDS, FOLKLORE, AND STORIES OF ANCIENT WORLDS

Titles
in the Series

The Life and Times of:

The Life and Times of

SOCRATES

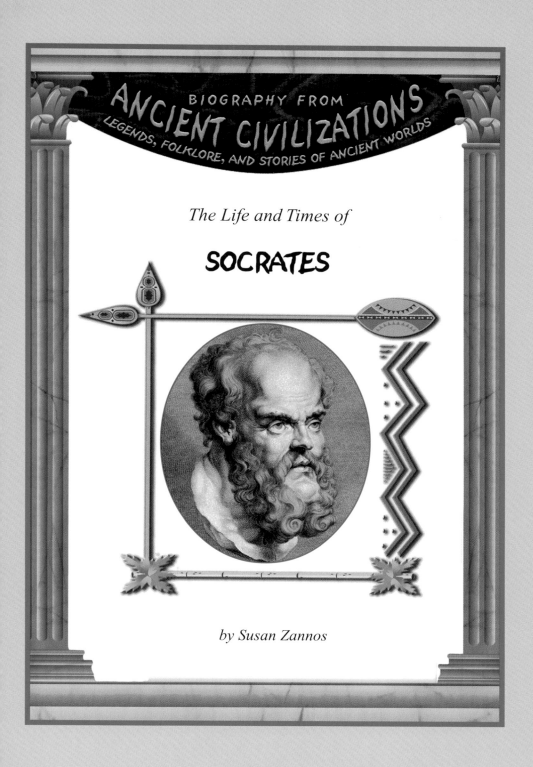

by Susan Zannos

Printing   2   3   4   5   6   7   8
Library of Congress Cataloging-in-Publication Data

Zannos, Susan.
    The life and times of Socrates / Susan Zannos.
        p. cm. — (Biography from ancient civilizations)
    Includes bibliographical references and index.
    ISBN 1-58415-282-6 (library bound)
    1. Socrates—Juvenile literature. I. Title. II. Series.
B316.Z36 2004
183'.2—dc22
                                                                        200400245

ABOUT THE AUTHOR: Susan Zannos has been a lifelong educator, having
taught at all levels, from preschool to college, in Mexico, Greece, Italy, Russia, and
Lithuania, as well as in the United States. She has published a mystery *Trust the Liar*
(Walker and Co.) and *Human Types: Essence and the Enneagram* (Samuel Weiser). Her
book, *Human Types*, was recently translated into Russian, and in 2003 Susan was
invited to tour Russia and lecture about her book. Another book she wrote for young
adults, *Careers in Education* (Mitchell Lane) was selected for the New York Public
Library's "Books for the Teen Age 2003 List." She has written many books for
children, including *Chester Carlson and the Development of Xerography* and *The Life and
Times of Ludwig van Beethoven* (Mitchell Lane). When not traveling, Susan lives in the
Sierra Foothills of Northern California.

PHOTO CREDITS: Cover, pp. 1, 3—Corbis (artist's conception); pp. 6, 20, 25,
30, 34, 36, 38—Hulton Archives/Getty Images; pp. 14, 16—Library of Congress;
p. 22—Superstock.

PUBLISHER'S NOTE: This story is based on the author's extensive research,
which she believes to be accurate. Documentation of such research is contained on
page 47. The stories in the Biography From Ancient Civilizations series take place
before the invention of photography. Therefore, no accurate images of the people
exist. Some artists' engravings, sculptures, and sketches have survived time. Some of
the images we have chosen to include may have been modified or colored for artistic
purposes only.

The internet sites referenced herein were active as of the publication date. Due to
the fleeting nature of some web sites, we cannot guarantee they will all be active
when you are reading this book.

BIOGRAPHY FROM
ANCIENT CIVILIZATIONS
LEGENDS, FOLKLORE, AND STORIES OF ANCIENT WORLDS

The Life and Times of

SOCRATES

            *FYI: For Your Information

In ancient Greece books were written by hand on scrolls. Although Socrates may have produced some written work when he was a young scholar, when he was older he did not write. His teaching was entirely spoken. The Socratic method was to confront his listeners with difficult questions. Others, such as his students Plato and Xenophon, wrote about Socrates' ideas after he had died.

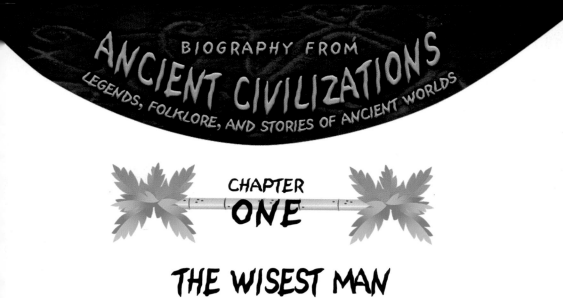

CHAPTER
ONE

THE WISEST MAN

Young Chaerephon followed the sun west from Athens, Greece, on his journey to the sacred shrine at Delphi. He was going to ask the oracle of Apollo whether any man was wiser than Socrates. When he reached the god's shrine at the foot of Mt. Parnassus, it was evening. The glow of the setting sun shone on the pillars of Apollo's temple and cast long shadows on the road. Eagerly, Chaerephon asked the attendant whether the priestess would answer questions the next day. He was delighted to learn that she would.

Apollo's priestess was called the Pythia. She delivered Apollo's words to those who came seeking advice. The god's words were always true, but sometimes confusing. They could be interpreted in different ways. Chaerephon hoped the answer to his question would be clear. He had been arguing with some of the young men of Athens. He was sure that his friend Socrates was the wisest of men. Some of the others didn't agree. They admired the Sophists, teachers who came to Athens from other parts of Greece. The Sophists specialized in clever speeches that twisted the meanings of words. They used tricks to convince their listeners.

Chaerephon and Socrates had been friends since they were boys. Chaerephon admired Socrates' brilliant mind, powers of reasoning, and scientific studies. He thought the Sophists were only playing word games, not presenting real knowledge. Next morning early, the eager young man again climbed the steep path to the temple, appreciating the treasuries containing the offerings that had been made to Apollo by the citizens of the different cities of Greece. He felt a rush of pride to see that the Athenian treasury held the richest and finest offerings of all.

When he reached the steps leading to Apollo's temple, Chaerephon turned and looked out over the magnificent view. Far down the mountainside he could see the glint of sunlight on the sea. There were only two men in front of him waiting to ask the Pythia their questions. As they waited, others joined them until there was quite a long line. When it was Chaerephon's turn, a priest led him to the altar, where he made a sacrifice of bay leaves and barley. Then they went down a flight of stairs that led beneath the temple. There, in a small chamber, the Pythia sat on a tall stool. She had a sprig of bay leaf in her hand. Her eyes seemed fixed and sightless. She was in her holy trance.

After she spoke the ritual words that welcomed Chaerephon, he blurted out his question: "Is there any man wiser than Socrates?"

The Pythia answered in one word. "No." She spoke no more.

Chaerephon could hardly wait to get back to Athens. When he did, he went immediately to find Socrates. He found him surrounded by a group of friends at one of their favorite hangouts, the shop of Simon the shoemaker near the cornerstone of the agora, the Athenian marketplace.

"What's happening?" Chaerephon asked someone standing in the doorway.

"Shhh, listen. Socrates and Critobulus are having a beauty contest."

Chaerephon burst out laughing. Critobulus was one of the handsomest young men in Athens. And even an admirer like Chaerephon had to admit that Socrates was not handsome. In fact, he was ugly. That brilliant logical mind was housed in a potbellied, spindly-legged body. Furthermore, his face featured a pug nose with flaring nostrils, bulging popped eyes, and thick rubbery lips. Nonetheless, Socrates was arguing that he was more beautiful than Critobulus.

Socrates began by asking Critobulus whether beauty is found only in men, and Critobulus answered that there are many different beautiful things, including animals, and swords and shields. When Socrates asked how it could be that things very different from each other could all be beautiful, Critobulus said that a thing was beautiful when it performed its function well.

Socrates then claimed that his eyes were more beautiful than Critobulus's eyes: "Because, while yours see only straight ahead, mine, by bulging out as they do, see also to the sides."[1]

"Well, let that pass," Critobulus said, "but whose nose is finer?"

"Mine, I consider," answered Socrates, "granting that Providence made us noses to smell with. For your nostrils look down toward the ground, but mine are wide open and turned outward so that I can catch scents from all about."[2]

By this time Critobulus was well aware that Socrates had trapped him as soon as he had said that beauty depended on function. Critobulus himself said, "As for the mouth, I concede that point. For if it is created for the purpose of biting off food, you could bite off a far bigger mouthful than I could. And don't you think that your kiss is also the more tender because you have thick lips?"

Critobulus said that he could not argue any longer, and that they should hand out the ballots so that everyone could vote on who was the more beautiful. In the end, no one voted for Socrates. Critobulus was declared the winner of their beauty contest in spite of Socrates' clever arguments. Socrates claimed that Critobulus must have bribed all the judges or he never would have won.

With much laughter and joking the group of young men continued their discussions. Talking and reasoning and arguing were their favorite pastimes. They gathered every day in the agora to talk and enjoy each other's company.

"Socrates," Chaerephon said when the beauty contest was over, "I have something important to tell you." He drew his friend out of the crowded shop and they walked together down the street. "I have just returned from Delphi. I consulted the oracle."

"And what did you have to ask Apollo?" Socrates asked in surprise.

"I asked if any man were wiser than you."

Socrates stopped and turned to his friend in amazement. "You did what?"

"I asked if any man were wiser than you, and the Pythia answered with one word. She said, 'No.'"

Socrates was rarely at a loss for words, but now he was stunned into silence. He was annoyed with his friend Chaerephon for what he had done. But the god's answer was far more shocking. Socrates, who was almost never away from the young men who spent their time together talking and exchanging ideas, now wanted to be alone.

Leaving Chaerephon and the agora behind, Socrates walked through the Kerameikos, the potters' district, and through the city gates. Outside the city was the outer Kerameikos, the cemetery. Through the tombs and gravestones ran a brook. As Socrates walked beside it, frogs plopped noisily into the water and tortoises lumbered through the tall grasses. The young philosopher was deep in thought.

Years and years later, just before his death, Socrates explained that the words of the Delphic oracle had changed his life. He said, "When I heard the answer, I asked myself: What can the god mean? What can he be hinting? For certainly I have never thought myself wise in anything, great or small. What can he mean then, when he asserts that I am the wisest of men? He cannot lie of course: that would be impossible for him. And for a long while I was at a loss to think what he could mean."[3]

In his effort to understand Apollo's answer to Chaerephon's question, Socrates began a search to find a man who was wiser

than he was. He went to a man who was considered one of the wisest in Athens, but when he talked to this man he realized that even though other people, and the man himself, thought he was wise, he really wasn't. Socrates tried to show the man that he wasn't really wise, but the man just got angry.

After that experience, Socrates went to another man who was considered to be wise. The same thing happened. The man became angry. In spite of the difficulties, Socrates continued: "Thus I went round them all, one after the other, aware of what was happening and sorry for it, and afraid that they were getting to hate me: but still I felt I must put the word of the god first and foremost, and that I must go through all who seemed to have any knowledge in order to find out what the oracle meant."[4]

Socrates questioned statesmen and writers and craftsmen. He made many bitter enemies as he refuted the ideas these men had. At last he decided: "The truth may be that God alone has wisdom, and by that oracle he may have meant just this, that human wisdom is of little or no account. It seems as though he had not been speaking of Socrates the individual; but had merely used my name for an illustration, as if to say: 'He, O men, is the wisest of you all, who has learnt, like Socrates, that his wisdom is worth nothing.' "[5]

Socrates considered that he had been given a sacred task by the god. He spent the rest of his life tirelessly fulfilling this task.

The Delphic Oracle

Apollo's temple in the sacred sanctuary at Delphi contained a special chamber deep in the earth. In this chamber the Pythia, a woman dedicated to Apollo to serve as his priestess, would sit on a tall tripod, or three-legged stool. People traveled from far and wide to ask questions of Apollo. In a trance, the Pythia would respond to their questions. This was the Delphic Oracle, the god Apollo speaking to humans through his priestess.

The Pythias purified themselves and drank pure waters from a spring that bubbled up inside the temple. On days when she answered questions, the priestess burned bay leaves and barley on the altar, and then sat on the high stool. When the god inspired her, people came in one at a time.

They spoke directly to the Pythia, and she answered them.

One ancient wise man, Heraclitus, observed, "No-where or ever did the God of Delphi either reveal or conceal. He indicates only." In other words, it was up to the person receiving the message to use his good judgment in applying the message. One king who wanted to attack a neighboring kingdom asked the oracle if he would succeed. He was told that if he attacked, he would destroy a mighty kingdom. The king, pleased with the message from the god, went to war. He did destroy a mighty kingdom, but it was his own.

In modern centuries people thought that the stories about the oracle at Delphi were only superstition. They thought the Pythia was faking her responses. In the last few years, however, scientists have found that the oracle chamber was built over geological fault lines from which escaped gases that cause a trance-like state. One of these gases, ethylene, is sweet-smelling like perfume. Ancient writers described this sweet smell in the oracle chamber. The scientists concluded: "God though he was, Apollo had to speak through the voices of mortals, and he had to inspire them with stimuli that were part of the natural world."

The Parthenon, the magnificent temple dedicated to the goddess Athena on the Acropolis of Athens, is considered one of the most perfect works of architecture ever created. Planned as part of the reconstruction of Athens after the Persians destroyed the old temples in 480 B.C., work on the Parthenon was directed by the sculptor Phidias. Although partially destroyed, this temple has stood proudly above Athens for 2,500 years.

CHAPTER TWO

THE GLORY THAT WAS GREECE

Socrates was born around 470 B.C., near the beginning of one of the most glorious periods in human history, the golden age of Greece. He did not come from a wealthy or noble family. His father, Sophroniscus, was a sculptor well respected in Athens. His mother, Phaenarete, was a midwife. The family lived in a stoneworkers' suburb on Mount Lykabettos, which is only about a 20-minute walk from the center of Athens.

Chaerephon, who tagged along after Socrates when they were boys, was one of his friends. From their neighborhood on Lykabettos, the boys could see the acropolis, the high city with its temples and walls. Socrates' father went there every day to work on the new building projects Pericles decreed. When he grew old enough, Socrates became his father's apprentice and learned stonecutting. A sculpture of the three Graces on the acropolis was said to be Socrates' work.

Very little is known about the early life of Socrates. Since he never wrote anything himself, all we know about him we learn from others who knew him and wrote about him. And even these

*The Acropolis (the word means "high city" in Greek) of
Athens was both a religious center of the city where there were
temples to the gods, and a fortress where the citizens could
retreat when enemies attacked the city. The Parthenon,
dedicated to the patron goddess of the city, Athena, can still be
seen on the Acropolis. In the middle ground are the columns
that are all that remain of the Zeus temple.*

few accounts tell us as much about the people who wrote them as
they do about Socrates. Each of the writers had his own purposes.
None of them intended to write a biography of Socrates.

The first to write about Socrates was Aristophanes, a comic
poet. His play *The Clouds* was a satire that made fun of Socrates
and his students. Of course, since it was a comedy, the purpose of
the play was to make people laugh. Aristophanes used
exaggeration and ridicule, so it is impossible to tell what aspects
of Socrates' character in the play are like the character of the
philosopher. But there must have been similarities or the
audience would not have recognized the comic portrait as that of
Socrates.

The next men to write about Socrates were both his students, and they didn't even meet him until he was over 50 years old. The two students, Plato and Xenophon, were very different, and their portraits of Socrates are also very different. Still, there are enough details that are the same to help us get a glimpse of some of the things Socrates did and said.

Plato was a philosopher himself. It is hard to tell when he is giving an accurate account of what Socrates said, and when he is using Socrates to present what are actually his own ideas. Xenophon was a soldier and later a gentleman farmer. His stories about Socrates intend to show that Socrates was a good citizen and a good teacher. Another person who wrote about Socrates was Plato's student Aristotle. His evaluation of Socrates seems the most objective, but he never actually knew Socrates.

Even though we don't know many details about Socrates' life when he was a young man, we do know quite a lot about what life in Athens was like. The events that inspired the brilliant achievements in Athens at this time were the defeat of the Persians at the battle of Marathon and Salamis. Athens and several other Greek city-states joined together to form the Delian League to protect themselves from Persian attacks. Each member of the league provided either ships or the money to build ships. Athens, under the leadership of the great statesman Pericles, was the strongest of the cities and the leader and treasurer of the alliance.

The wealth and power of Athens attracted the best minds and talents of Greece. They also attracted the worst minds, every kind of con man and charlatan. Pericles, whose goal was to make his city the greatest in the world, welcomed scientists and artists, astronomers and mathematicians, musicians and poets to Athens.

His building projects were aimed at making Athens the most beautiful as well as the most powerful city.

In spite of the work available for stonecutters and sculptors, Socrates must have given up his trade very early. The hammer and chisel could not compete with philosophy. The word *philosophy* (which comes from Greek) means "love of wisdom." It was not knowledge that Socrates was after, but wisdom. Although he studied science for a while when he was young, it didn't interest him for long.

From his youth, Socrates wanted to answer big questions: *What does it mean to be a good man? What is happiness? What is justice? What is man's relationship to the gods?* There were many in Athens who thought they had the answers to these questions. Socrates sought them out, questioned them, argued with them, and came away dissatisfied with their answers.

Because of his intense interest in discussions, many considered Socrates to be one of the Sophists. Sophists were lecturers and teachers who charged money to teach young men how to speak well and influence people. One of the earliest Sophists was Corax of Syracuse. He even wrote a book about how to persuade people, and he called this practice "rhetoric" (we still use this word to refer to the effective use of language).

Corax had a student, Tisias, who took his course but refused to pay the fee. Corax took his student to court, where Tisias said, "Before I started, you promised you would teach me to persuade anyone to do whatever I wanted. Let me now persuade you not to ask for your fee. If you still demand it, you did not do what you promised, therefore I owe you nothing."[1]

With people using the techniques of the Sophists this way—to avoid paying their debts or to break the law and get away with it—it is not surprising that many people thought that all Sophists were cheats and liars. True, some were. But not all.

Zeno of Elea was a brilliant Sophist who could prove any proposition to be false. One of his most famous proofs was that Achilles, one of the fastest runners of all time, could not pass a turtle. If the turtle was 100 yards ahead of Achilles, by the time Achilles reached that spot the turtle would have moved a few feet, and by the time Achilles reached that spot the turtle would have moved a bit farther, and so forth. So Achilles could never pass the turtle.

Zeno visited Athens when Socrates was a young man and, according to Plato, Socrates met him at this time. Another great scientist and thinker who came to Athens, and who influenced Pericles, was Anaxagoras. At a time when it was believed that the sun and moon were gods, Anaxagoras dared to say that the moon had hills and valleys like the earth, and that it shone with reflected light. He furthermore said that the sun was a very hot rock. For such disrespect to the gods he was banished from Athens, but not before he had a profound effect on the questioning mind of young Socrates.

After Anaxagoras was forced to leave Athens, his students were taught by his successor, Archelaus, who was for many years the teacher and close friend of Socrates. After Archelaus retired, Socrates became the leader of the associates who studied together. It is this way that we see him and his students satirized by the comic poet Aristophanes in *The Clouds*.

According to legend, a messenger ran about 20 miles from the battlefield at Marathon to Athens to announce the stunning victory of the Athenian army over the invading Persians, then died from his efforts. While no one knows if this actually happened, the legend was so well-known that the revival of the Olympic Games in 1896 included a marathon run. The official distance of the race became fixed at 26.2 miles early in the twentieth century.

The Athens of Socrates' youth and young manhood was a far different place than the Athens of his old age. Prosperous and powerful, Athens during the golden age witnessed the building of the Parthenon and other temples; the sculptures of Phidias and other great artists that adorned the temples; the plays of Aeschylus, Sophocles, and Euripides that were performed at the great religious festivals. But this amazing flowering of creativity was brief. Although it would influence all of Western civilization, it lasted barely 50 years. By the time Socrates was 40 years old, the glory that was Greece was ending. Replacing the great art created in a time of pride and achievement came the great age of philosophy, born of disillusion and defeat.

The Persian Wars

By about 500 B.C., the Persian Empire had conquered all of the lands of the eastern Mediterranean. The Persian king, Darius 1, was angry because the Athenians had supported the revolt of Ionian cities against Persia. He led his army to attack Athens.

The huge Persian army of 48,000 men landed at Marathon, 26 miles northeast of Athens, on September 9, 490 B.C. On the hillside above the plain of Marathon, 11,000 Greeks waited. They were outnumbered four to one. As the Persians advanced, the Athenians charged toward them, managed to surround them, and drove them back to their ships. While the Persians fled and the Athenians pursued them, 192 Greek soldiers died. The Persian casualties numbered 6,400.

Seven Persian ships were destroyed. The Athenian general, Miltiades, realized that the rest of the Persian ships could sail around and attack Athens. He asked the fastest Greek runner to run the 26 miles to Athens, tell them of the victory, and warn them that the Persians were coming. The valiant runner completed his task in about three hours. After fighting all day and making the run to warn the Athenians, he died of exhaustion. When the Persians arrived and saw the Athenians armed for battle, they turned and sailed back to Persia.

Despite their defeat at Marathon, the Persians were determined to conquer Greece. By 480 B.C. King Xerxes, son of Darius, had an army of 150,000 men and a navy of 600 ships. Athens, Sparta, and 29 other city-states joined forces to fight the Persians.

The Athenians began building ships while a group of 300 Spartans made their stand at a narrow pass through the mountains at Thermopylae. The Spartans sacrificed themselves to give the Athenians time to complete the ships. The Persians attacked again and again, but the Spartans trapped them in the narrow pass and drove them back until all the Spartans were killed. Xerxes pushed on and burned Athens.

The great naval battle that ended the Persian Wars was the battle of Salamis. The Persian ships outnumbered the Greek ships three to one, and Xerxes expected to win easily. But the Greek ships were smaller and faster. They lured the Persian ships into the narrow strait between the mainland and the island of Salamis. The faster Greek ships rammed the clumsy Persian war galleys. About 200 Persian ships were sunk, others were captured, and the rest fled back to Persia.

Socrates was a well-known figure in the Athenian agora, the busy marketplace at the foot of the acropolis. Barefoot, poorly dressed, usually accompanied by a group of young men who were his students, he would approach anyone who passed, powerful politicians or simple laborers, and ask them questions about their opinions and beliefs. He referred to himself as "the gadfly of the state." This is one artist's conception of what Socrates might have looked like.

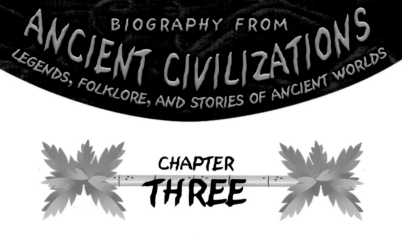

CHAPTER
THREE

THE YOUNG PHILOSOPHER

The comic play by Aristophanes that makes fun of Socrates also shows a lot about the life of the young philosopher. In *The Clouds,* the main character is a foolish old man who goes to Socrates' school because he wants to learn how to cheat the people he owes money to. Much of the comedy results from the old man's inability to learn even the simplest things in spite of Socrates' attempts to teach him.

Even in the comedy, the character Socrates does not help the old man to cheat people. He tries to teach the foolish man to think correctly. Unfortunately he fails. In the play, Socrates and his students are very poor and living together in Socrates' house. From this we know that at one time, while he was still a young man, Socrates was the teacher, or at least the leader, of a group of serious students.

The fact that Aristophanes chose Socrates as the subject of his comedy shows that Socrates was widely known as an intellectual. In Aristophanes' play the students have maps and tools for the study of geography, geology, and astronomy. This would indicate that when he was younger, Socrates studied the sciences. Later he would give this up to devote all his time to philosophy.

The one thing that seems the same from his early years to his old age was that Socrates had no interest in material things. He refused to work at anything that would earn money. Even when many young men gathered around him to learn from him, he never charged money for his teaching. His clothes were ragged and he wore the same shabby cloak summer and winter. He wore no shoes, even when it was very cold in the winter.

One of the Sophists wanted to attract the men who studied with Socrates. He wanted them to become his students and pay him money. He made fun of the poverty in which Socrates lived and said, "You must consider yourself but a teacher of wretchedness."[1]

In response Socrates said that he was better off than a wealthy man. He enjoyed food more because he didn't have much of it. He was stronger and healthier because he was not affected by either heat or cold. Socrates said, "I think that to want nothing is to resemble the gods, and that to want as little as possible is to make the nearest approach to the gods."[2] Throughout his life, Socrates insisted that happiness does not come from having more. It comes from wanting less.

Socrates also argued that he was better prepared than other men to be a soldier, since he would not miss rich food and drink, but could survive on very little. And he was used to heat and cold and being uncomfortable. Before too long he had a chance to prove that this was true. By the time Socrates was 40 years old,

Socrates accepted no payment from the young men who gathered around him and chose him as their teacher. He taught them no principles or doctrines except that they must not accept any principles or doctrines without examining them and questioning them and finding out for themselves what they believed.

there was a war between Athens and Sparta. The ruler in Athens, Pericles, tried to keep people calm, but there were many who thought Athens was so powerful that Sparta could not harm her. War started between these two most powerful Greek city-states in 431 B.C.

Despite his age, Socrates served as a hoplite in at least three battles of the war with Sparta. The hoplites formed the most important part of the Greek army. They were infantrymen who wore heavy armor and carried a shield and spear into battle. If the spear broke, they also had a sword. The hoplites were citizens who provided their own armaments. The fact that Socrates was a hoplite shows that he could afford to buy his own armor, which was expensive. From this we know that he was not as poor as his clothing and simple living made people think. He chose that way of life. And when he felt his duty was to defend Athens, he chose to fight as a hoplite.

The hoplites fought in close ranks about eight rows deep. Their shields were designed so that each one protected the left side of the man carrying it and the right side of the man next to him. Fighting was definitely a social affair. A man's honor depended on not breaking ranks. The opposing lines of soldiers would crash into each other, trying to break through the enemy's lines. The men behind the front lines pushed the men in the front line forward, and they took the place of any comrades who fell under the enemy's spears.

The first battle in which Socrates was known to have fought was at Potidaea, the first battle of the Second Peloponnesian War, the second war between Athens and Sparta. At Potidaea, Socrates fought beside his young student Alcibiades, who later told how Socrates saved his life when he was wounded. "It was entirely to Socrates that I owed my preservation," said Alcibiades; "he would not leave me when I was wounded, but succeeded in rescuing both me and my arms."[3]

After three years of fighting, Socrates returned to Athens, which was suffering from a terrible plague. (Pericles lost his entire family in the plague and in 429 B.C. died from it himself.) In six more years Socrates again took up his hoplite armor to fight at Delium, where Athens was badly defeated.

Alcibiades was again in the same battle. He described Socrates "strutting along with his head in the air and casting sidelong glances, making it perfectly plain even at a distance that he was prepared to put up a strong resistance to any attack. That is how both he and his companion got off safe; those who show a bold front in war are hardly ever molested."[4] Two years after that, Socrates saw action again in the north when Sparta attacked Thrace, Athens' ally.

His military service was not a great disturbance to Socrates' life. As he pointed out in his argument with the Sophist, he was accustomed to going without fancy food and drink, and he was used to discomfort from heat and cold. And we can hardly suppose that he stopped talking and asking questions and arguing just because he was in the army. The other hoplites probably got their share of difficult discussions.

Socrates had other odd characteristics besides his appearance and his shabby clothing. One of these was his habit of going into a trance-like state when he was thinking about a problem. His friends reported that he sometimes would stand motionless for hours, sometimes missing appointments or meals. At Potidaea he once began thinking about some problem at around sunrise. He stood all day in the same place, thinking. When night fell the other soldiers began gathering around to see how long this strange man would stand there motionless. He stood there all night. When the sun came up the next morning, he made his sacrifice to the gods and went about his business.

Another oddity was what he called his daemon. This was evidently a warning voice; not exactly a guardian angel, but something like it. According to his reports, this daemon did not tell him what to do, but what not to do. If people were urging a particular course of action, and that action would lead to disaster, Socrates' daemon would tell him not to follow that action. One thing it told him was to stay out of politics. This was excellent advice—and except for a brief stint in 406 B.C. as a member of the Boule, the legislative body of Athens, it was advice he followed.

The political situation in Athens was extremely unstable. Without the leadership of Pericles there were disagreements about what to do. For six years there was a truce with Sparta. Then in 415 B.C. the ambitious Alcibiades, the same man whose life Socrates had saved, convinced the Athenians to attack the city-states on the island of Sicily. With these cities under the control of Athens, Alcibiades argued, Athens would be invincible.

The expedition was a disaster. The Athenian army was defeated, and most of the fleet was destroyed in Sicily's harbor of Syracuse.

Sparta, seeing Athens helpless, soon attacked. Alcibiades turned traitor and fled to Sparta, where he helped in the final defeat of Athens in 404 B.C. The Spartans tore down the city walls, forbade the Athenians to build ships, and installed their own government, the Thirty Tyrants. Socrates had good reason to regret he had taught Alcibiades how to persuade people.

Pericles

The great Athenian statesman Pericles was born in 495 B.C. His family, on both his father's and his mother's side, was among the wealthiest in Athens. Pericles was a powerful speaker and his skill with words made him famous. He was dignified and calm in all his actions.

Pericles had one passion: his love of Athens. When he entered politics, it was with the aim of making Athens the greatest and most beautiful city in the world. His success was the amazing 50-year period that is known as the golden age of Greece. The art, architecture, drama, religious festivals, philosophy, and government of the Age of Pericles formed the foundation for Western civilization.

Pericles was first elected general in 460 B.C., and he was regularly reelected for 30 years. At a time when most Greek city-states were ruled by kings or tyrants, Pericles created democracy in Athens. All of the citizens voted and lived under the rule of law.

The Greeks formed the Delian League, which was a group of city-states that joined together for mutual defense against Persia. The powerful Persian Empire, which had threatened the Greeks for years, was finally defeated. Once the danger was past, Pericles used the money from the league's treasury for building projects in Athens, such as the magnificent temple of Athena, the Parthenon. The other city-states were not happy with this arrangement, but since Athens was by far the most powerful state, they couldn't do much about it.

Soon, however, Sparta and some other cities revolted against Athens. The final years of Pericles' life were full of struggle and tragedy as Athens was defeated from without by Sparta and from within by a terrible plague. The disease killed all of Pericles' family and in 429 B.C. killed him as well. The glory that was Greece slipped into history.

Of all Pericles' speeches, only one remains: the funeral oration he delivered in honor of the dead during the first year of the war with Sparta. In it he said, "Of all cities, Athens alone is even greater than her fame. . . . Her enemies when defeated are not disgraced; her subjects confess that she is worthy to rule them." Of those who had died in the war, he said, "To men who fall as they have fallen, death is no evil."

Socrates observed that happiness is gained not by having more but by wanting less. He taught this by example as well as by words. He dressed very simply, not even wearing a heavy cloak in cold weather, and had very few possessions. He would walk through the agora, the Athenian marketplace, looking in the shops and saying, "Look at all the things that Socrates doesn't need!"

CHAPTER
FOUR

THE EXAMINED LIFE

Plato was 20 years old when he finally met Socrates. He had already heard about the eccentric philosopher from his older brothers and his uncle. After the death of Socrates 20 years later, Plato began writing his famous dialogues. Socrates was the central figure in many of these works. These dialogues are so interesting that they have remained popular for over two thousand years.

In Athenian society, love between men was not only accepted but also believed to be the highest form of love. Even though men had wives and families, their social lives were spent in the company of other men. The status of women in Athens was very low. Women were considered little more than servants and were not seen outside the home or even in the social rooms of their own houses. Perhaps this was one reason why men chose young men rather than women for lovers.

When he returned from the wars with Sparta, Socrates married. His wife, Xanthippe, had the reputation of being a nag with a violent temper. Once when he was asked why he had married such a woman, Socrates said that it was his aim to be able to get along with everyone. He said that he married Xanthippe because he knew she was difficult and he could practice on her. They had three sons. Being married to Socrates could not have been easy for Xanthippe. With three small children to raise and a husband who refused to work to support them, it is no wonder the poor woman had a bad disposition.

Socrates (and his student Plato after him) did not emphasize physical love. He was concerned with spiritual and emotional love—friendship between equals and tender care for the young boys entering manhood.

Many of the early Socratic dialogues that Plato wrote are about young men and their education. They raise questions about the nature of ideals, such as bravery, happiness, and goodness. The questions are often not answered. Socrates did not have a morality that he preached. His purpose was to get people to examine the questions themselves. He thought that people too often simply accepted the ideas of their families, or of political leaders, without thinking about the ideas for themselves.

One of the most famous quotations from Socrates says, "The unexamined life is not worth living." A good example of a dialogue in which Socrates raises questions about friendship and love is Plato's *Lysis*, one of the early dialogues. Socrates, the narrator, is out walking when he is invited by a friend to visit the wrestling school and meet the handsome young Lysis. Socrates demonstrates the highest kind of friendship or love by his method of teaching Lysis.

"I suppose, Lysis," Socrates says, "your father and mother love you very much?"

"Of course," he replied.

"Then they'd want you to be as happy as possible?"

"Naturally."

"Do you think that a man is happy when he's a slave and allowed to do nothing he desires?"

"Heavens, no, I don't," he said.[1]

Socrates then says that if Lysis's parents want him to be happy, they must let him do whatever he wants and never scold him or prevent him from doing things. The boy admits that they do in fact stop him from doing many things, and that he has to follow many rules. The two of them talk about the things Lysis is not allowed to do, such as drive his father's chariot in a race, and the things he is allowed to do, such as tune his own lyre (a stringed musical instrument) before he plays it.

They agree that the things Lysis is free to do are things about which he has knowledge. From there they agree that it is knowledge that gives one freedom, and someone who loves another will educate him so he can be free and therefore happy.

After talking about the love of a parent for a child, the group begins talking of friendship and the kind of love friends have for each other. Socrates tells the boys that he's always desired to have friends, but he doesn't know how one man becomes the friend of another. From then on they explore many different aspects of friendship, but never arrive at any conclusions before the boys' tutors come and call them home.

It seems clear that Socrates' intention was not to lead the boys to a particular understanding, but to lead them to examine their own feelings and ideas. He wanted them to be not only good friends, but good philosophers as well.

Hoplites, the Greek foot soldiers, were citizens who provided their own armor and weapons, which included helmets and shields, spears and swords. They marched in close formation, creating a wall of shields with which they forced the enemy back. The bonds hoplites formed with their fellow soldiers made them courageous in protecting each other.

Plato also wrote dialogues in which Socrates was not at all gentle in his questions. In some of the dialogues in which Socrates is talking to Sophists such as Gorgias or Hippias, he is very ironic in his questions. He is actually making fun of these men, but they are so vain and sure of themselves that they do not realize that Socrates is destroying their opinions with his clever arguments.

Although many of his admirers urged Socrates to go into politics, he refused. He said that his daemon, that inner voice that told him what not to do, warned him against it. Instead he followed what he understood to be the task given him by the god Apollo. He spent his time walking the streets of the Athenian agora, talking and questioning. He argued with generals and politicians. He spoke with merchants and craftsmen. He questioned poets and artists and sculptors. He talked to athletes and soldiers.

Everyone knew Socrates. Not everyone liked him. The men that he showed to be hypocrites and liars hated him. But the young men admired him. They would gather around eagerly when Socrates got into a conversation with one of the politicians or Sophists or generals. And they would laugh when Socrates confused his opponents and made them admit that their beliefs were ridiculous.

Socrates would not charge money for the lessons he showed his young followers, but they were his students nonetheless. Some of them, like Plato and Xenophon, were serious young men who shared Socrates' search for answers to questions about how it was best for men to live their lives. Others, however, were ambitious and greedy. They saw that Socrates could defeat anyone in an argument with his clever reasoning. They wanted to learn how he managed to convince people. They wanted to use his techniques for their own gain.

Socrates was as brave defending the laws of Athens as he had been fighting as a hoplite in the battles against Sparta. On one occasion when he had court duty, the government demanded that the court condemn to death all of the eight captains who had fought in a sea battle with Sparta. The citizens were outraged because the captains had not taken time after the battle to rescue the soldiers who had fallen into the sea. They left the men to drown. Socrates, alone of those serving in the court, refused to vote against the captains. Athenian law required that each man be tried separately. Socrates said that it was illegal to condemn the captains as a group. The citizens of Athens were furious, but Socrates would not change his vote. It did no good, because the captains were executed anyway.

The Spartans had fought beside the Athenians to defeat the Persians, but when the Persian Wars were over these two great city states warred with each other. Sparta was a military state that trained its soldiers from childhood. The Spartans defeated the Athenians and tore down the walls of Athens.

Before vengeance was taken on Socrates by the Athenian democracy, the government of Athens changed. In 404 B.C. Sparta completely defeated Athens, tore down the city walls, and chose their own government, the Thirty Tyrants. Critias, a relative of Socrates, was among the worst of the tyrants. And Socrates' uncle, Charmides, was also active in the new government.

Once again Socrates defied the orders of the government. The tyrants ordered him and three or four other men to arrest a wealthy man, Leon of Salamis. The tyrants wanted to seize Leon's property. The other men did what they were told. Socrates simply went home. Leon was put to death. Socrates expected that he himself would be executed for his disobedience. But before that could happen there was a revolution that ended the cruelties of the Thirty Tyrants. They were put to death and democracy was restored in Athens.

Sparta

The two greatest city-states in ancient Greece were Athens and Sparta. Although they were both Greek, they were very different. After the Persians were defeated, Athens and Sparta became bitter enemies in a disastrous war, called the Peloponnesian War. Sparta defeated Athens.

By the eighth century B.C. Sparta was growing. Because they lived in a mountainous region, the Spartans needed land that could be farmed. They invaded their neighbors, the Messenians, who lived on a fertile plain. In the following century, the Messenians revolted and almost destroyed Sparta. Realizing that they were constantly in danger from this conquered people, who outnumbered them ten to one, the Spartans created a military state and made agricultural slaves out of the Messenians.

While Athens created a democracy that was controlled by its citizens, Sparta created a state that completely controlled its citizens. When a child was born, the state decided whether it was strong and healthy enough to live. If not, the infant was left out in the mountains to die. When Spartan boys were seven years old, they were put in military and athletic schools that taught them discipline and survival and resistance to pain. When the young men reached the age of 20 they became soldiers.

Not until he was 30 years old did the Spartan have his own house where he could live with his wife and children, although he still was a soldier. Each Spartan soldier was given land. Messenian slaves farmed his land. The Spartan's life was highly disciplined.

When the other Greek city-states began coining money to make buying and selling easier, the Spartan king, Lycurgus, wondered if Sparta should have its own money. He was afraid that if the Spartans had money, they would become lazy and luxury-loving like the citizens of many other city-states. Lycurgus's solution was to make the Spartan money out of heavy bars of iron. It was so heavy to carry around that the Spartans didn't bother with it for trivial purchases.

Spartan women were also given an education that emphasized physical development and service to the state. They did not have military training, but they had more freedom to manage their homes than any other Greek women. A Spartan wife or mother would tell her husband or son when he went to war, "Return with your shield or upon it." She meant that it was better to die a hero's death and be carried home on his shield than to be a coward in battle.

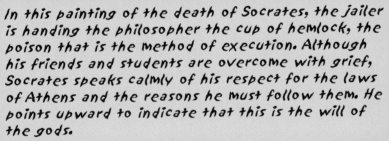

In this painting of the death of Socrates, the jailer is handing the philosopher the cup of hemlock, the poison that is the method of execution. Although his friends and students are overcome with grief, Socrates speaks calmly of his respect for the laws of Athens and the reasons he must follow them. He points upward to indicate that this is the will of the gods.

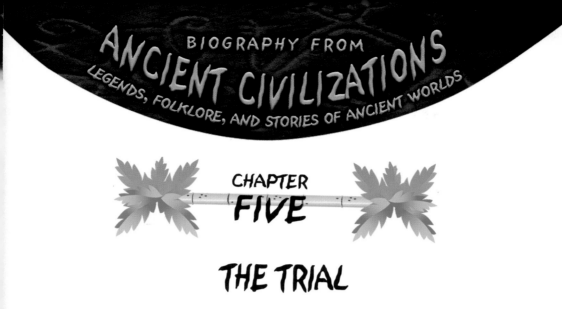

CHAPTER
FIVE

THE TRIAL

When the Athenian democracy was again formed in 403 B.C., and the Thirty Tyrants executed, an amnesty was declared. This was done so that past conflicts could be forgotten and the different parties in Athens could work together to rebuild their city. They began to revise the laws. It took them three years.

Athens was no longer the great and proud city it had been when Socrates was a young man. Some of the best-known politicians, like Alcibiades and Critias, had proved to be traitors helping Sparta. Many of the young men of Athens had died in the wars. A third of the population had died in the terrible plague that attacked the city from inside the walls while Sparta attacked from outside.

As often happens when troubles and suffering occur, the Athenians looked for someone to blame. Socrates, who had made many enemies with his questioning of public men and criticism of public policies, was accused of not worshiping the official gods of Athens, and for corrupting the young men. The prosecutor demanded the death penalty.

It was not clear exactly what the charges against Socrates meant. Perhaps they really didn't mean anything except that Socrates was considered a troublemaker. The new political leaders did not want to hear his critical comments about them.

According to historian A. E. Taylor, "The object of demanding the death sentence was merely to induce Socrates to consult his own safety by withdrawing into exile and letting the case go by default."[1] What the politicians wanted was for Socrates to get out of town and leave them alone. But Socrates wouldn't leave.

When his friends urged him to go to save his life, he refused. He said that he had always obeyed the laws of Athens and he would continue to obey them. If the law charged him with crimes, then he would stand trial.

The two charges against Socrates, that of introducing new gods and that of corrupting the youth, were never clearly presented by the prosecution. The first one may have referred to earlier days when Socrates was influenced by Anaxagoras. This early astronomer had been exiled for saying the sun and moon were not gods. Also, in Aristophanes' play *The Clouds*, Socrates is shown studying science and saying that it is not Zeus that creates thunder and lightning—it is the clouds. From this the comic poet showed Socrates to be saying that the clouds were gods. Although these things had occurred over 25 years earlier, it was against the new laws of Athens to worship any gods but the official ones.

The second charge, corrupting young men, also could not be openly presented because of the amnesty. People were angry about the crimes of Alcibiades and Critias, both of whom had been close friends of Socrates. They felt that Socrates had influenced these traitors.

Although the charges were not clear, Socrates understood perfectly well what was behind them. The jury at his trial was composed of 500 citizens—it was essentially a public trial. Socrates spoke about his reputation for teaching strange things. He said it was nonsense. He told of his mission, given to him by the god Apollo, to see if he could find a man wiser than himself.

He then said, "I have never been any man's teacher." He went on to say he had never taken payment from anyone but had never prevented anyone from listening to him if they wanted to. "And for that," he said, "if anyone is the better and anyone the worse, I ought not to be held responsible; I never promised instruction, I never taught, and if any man says he has ever learnt or heard one word from me in private other than all the world could hear, I tell you he does not speak the truth."[2]

If he was not a teacher, Socrates went on to ask, why did some men like to follow him around and listen to him? He said that they liked "hearing men examined who thought that they were wise but were not so; and certainly it is not unpleasant."[3]

Socrates ended his defense, which is recorded in Plato's dialogue "The Apology," by saying that he was not going to plead for his life and beg for mercy as some men did. He said such behavior brought shame upon the city because cases should be decided according to law, not as personal favors.

The jury of 500 voted by a majority of 60 votes that Socrates was guilty.

The next step in the process, according to Athenian law, was for the accused to offer an alternate punishment. The usual practice was to choose banishment rather than death. But again Socrates refused to do what was expected of him.

Instead of proposing a punishment, Socrates told the jury that he deserved to be rewarded for his services to the city. "What do I deserve to receive because I did not sit quiet all my life, and turned aside from what most men care for—money-making and household affairs, leadership in war and public speaking, and all the offices and associations and factions of the State? I should have been of no use there to you or to myself, but I set about going in private to each individual man and doing him the greatest of all services . . . trying to persuade every one of you not to think of what he had but rather of what he was, and how he might grow wise and good."[4]

For the service he had given Athens, Socrates proposed that he should be given the privilege of meals for life at the public table. This was an honor conferred upon such heroes as the winners at Olympic Games or famous generals. He also said that a fine was not evil if a man has money to pay it. He offered a ridiculously small amount, but said that his friends wanted to pay the fine for him.

A great many of the 500 jurors were enraged by Socrates' claim that he should be rewarded rather than punished. A much larger majority voted for the death penalty than had voted him guilty of the charges.

After being given the death penalty, Socrates told his judges that at no point did his daemon, the warning voice that stopped him if he was about to do any harm, try to stop him. He believed, therefore, that the death he faced could be a good thing. He said, "But now it is time for us to go, I to death, and you to life; and which of us goes to the better state is known to none but God."[5]

Socrates remained in prison for a month before he was executed. During that time his friends were able to visit him. They urged him to escape to save his life, and even convinced the jailer to help them. Socrates refused. His wife, Xanthippe, came to see him, but she cried and carried on so emotionally that Socrates asked her to leave.

On the last day of his life Socrates was as calm and cheerful as on any other day. He bathed and prepared himself so that others would not have to clean his body after his death. At sunset, the jailer brought hemlock, the poison that was the method of execution. Many of his friends began to cry, and one said that Socrates was innocent. In reply Socrates asked if his friends would prefer that he was guilty.

He drank the hemlock as the jailer instructed, walked around until his feet and legs began to feel heavy, and then lay down. The poison caused coldness in his arms and legs. As it approached his heart, Socrates covered his head with a cloth and peacefully died.

The ideals of the Greeks were expressed in their art and architecture, in poetry and dance and music. But most of all, the Greeks' continuing gift to humanity was philosophy. With his questions and arguments, his insistence on searching for truth, Socrates set all of Western history on the course it has taken for over two thousand years.

FYI
For Your Info

The Parthenon

The Parthenon was the temple of the goddess Athena on the acropolis. The acropolis, the high city, was a natural fortress in the center of Athens. Its sheer rock walls could withstand any attacking army. By the fifth century B.C., the acropolis had already been the site of temples and palaces for over a thousand years.

Pericles, the great Athenian statesman, planned the construction of new temples for the acropolis after the old ones were destroyed by the Persians in 480 B.C. The Parthenon was built first. Work began in 447 B.C. and lasted 15 years. All the Greek temples were built to house a god or goddess; the Parthenon was built to contain the cult statue of the goddess Athena, patron goddess of Athens.

The sculptor Phidias had artistic control of the project. He carved the 40-foot-tall statue of Athena from gold and ivory, and he supervised the construction of the temple to house the statue. The Parthenon had eight columns at each end instead of six like other temples. The long sides had seventeen columns, twice the number of the columns at the ends plus one more.

Because columns that were exactly the same diameter from top to bottom would appear to be smaller in the middle, the architects created columns that bulged out slightly in the middle so that they would appear straight. The architects designed the floor to curve up slightly in the middle so that the lines would appear to be horizontal.

At either end of the temple, above the columns that supported the roof, was a triangular stone called a pediment. Each pediment was decorated with three-dimensional figures representing a story. The east end of the Parthenon portrayed the birth of Athena from the head of Zeus. The west end showed the battle between Athena and Poseidon, god of the sea, who fought over who would be the patron deity of Athens. Some of these statues have been moved from the original site; they can be seen in the British Museum in London.

The remains of the Parthenon still stand on the acropolis in Athens. Throughout the centuries it served as a Christian church, as an Islamic mosque, and, unfortunately, as a storage place for munitions during a war. When a shell exploded, so did the rest of the explosives stored there, blowing the roof off and destroying much of the temple. But enough remains to attract thousands every year.

Chronology

All dates B.C.
470—Socrates born just outside of Athens
442—Delphic Oracle says that Socrates is the wisest man alive
430—serves in Peloponnesian War; saves Alcibiades at battle of Potidaea
423—Aristophanes writes *The Clouds,* a comedy satirizing Socrates
419—marries Xanthippe; they have three sons over the next 10 years
406—serves as member of the Boule, the legislative body of Athens
404—refuses order of the Thirty Tyrants to arrest Leon of Salamis
399—brought to trial on charges of impiety and corruption of youth; sentenced to death by taking hemlock

Timeline in History

490—Athenians defeat the Persians at Marathon.
480—Athens, Sparta, and 29 other Greek city-states unite to defeat the Persians at the battle of Salamis.
470—Socrates is born.
468—Aeschylus, the first great tragic poet, is at the height of his career.
460—First Peloponnesian War begins. Hippocrates, father of medicine, is born.
447—Construction of the Parthenon begins on the Athens acropolis.
445—First Peloponnesian War ends.
441—Revolt of Samos breaks peace in Aegean.
431—Second Peloponnesian War between Athens and Sparta begins.
429—Pericles dies.
428—Anaxagoras, first Athenian philosopher and teacher of Pericles and Socrates, dies.
415—Athens launches disastrous expedition to conquer Sicily.
404—Second Peloponnesian War ends in defeat of Athens by Sparta; Thirty Tyrants control Athens.
403—Thirty Tyrants deposed; democracy is restored.
400—Laws are reformed and general amnesty granted.
399—Socrates is tried and sentenced to death.
387—Plato founds his Academy in Athens.
335—Aristotle founds the Lyceum in Athens, a rival school to Plato's Academy.

Chapter Notes

CHAPTER ONE   THE WISEST MAN

1. Anthony Gottlieb, *Socrates* (London: Orion Publishing Group, Ltd., 1997), p. 7.

2. Ibid., p. 8.

3. Plato, "The Apology," *Socratic Discourses* (London: J.M. Dent & Sons, Ltd., Everyman's Library, 1944), p. 325.

4. Ibid., p. 326.

5. Ibid., p. 328.

CHAPTER TWO   THE GLORY THAT WAS GREECE

1. Pearl Cleveland Wilson, *The Living Socrates* (Owings Mills, MD: Stemmer House Publishers, Inc., 1975), p. 25.

CHAPTER THREE   THE YOUNG PHILOSOPHER

1. Xenophon, "Memorabilia," *Socratic Discourses* (London: J.M. Dent & Sons, Ltd., Everyman's Library, 1944), p. 30.

2. Ibid., p. 32.

3. Plato, *The Symposium* (London: Penguin Books, 1987), p. 109.

4. Ibid., p. 110.

CHAPTER FOUR   THE EXAMINED LIFE

1. Plato, *Early Socratic Dialogues* (London: Penguin Books, 1987), p. 169.

CHAPTER FIVE   THE TRIAL

1. A. E. Taylor, *Socrates, the Man and His Thought* (Garden City, NY: Garden City Press, 1954), p. 102.

2. Plato, "The Apology," *Socratic Discourses* (London: J.M. Dent & Sons, Ltd., Everyman's Library, 1944), p. 339-340.

3. Ibid., p. 340.

4. Ibid., p. 343.

5. Ibid., p. 349.

For Further Reading

For Young Adults

Gottlieb, Anthony. *Socrates*. London: Orion Publishing Group, Ltd., 1997.

Strathern, Paul. *Socrates in 90 Minutes*. Chicago: Ivan R. Dee, 1997.

Wilson, Pearl Cleveland. *The Living Socrates*. Owings Mills, MD: Stemmer House Publishers, Inc., 1975.

Works Consulted

Aristophanes. *The Frogs and Three Other Plays*. London: J.M. Dent & Sons, Ltd. Everyman's Library, 1945.

Gulley, Norman. *The Philosophy of Socrates*. New York: St. Martin's Press, 1968.

Guthrie, W.K.C. *Socrates*. Cambridge: Cambridge University Press, 1971.

Plato. *Early Socratic Dialogues*. London: Penguin Books, 1987.

Plato. *The Last Days of Socrates*, ed. Hugh Tredennick. New York: Penguin, 1995.

Plato. *The Symposium*. London: Penguin Books, 1987.

Plato and Xenophon. *Socratic Discourses*. London: J.M. Dent & Sons, Ltd., Everyman's Library, 1944.

Sauvage, Micheline. *Socrates and the Conscience of Man*. New York: Harper & Brothers, 1960.

Strauss, Leo. *Socrates and Aristophanes*. Chicago: University of Chicago Press, 1966.

Taylor, A. E. *Socrates, the Man and His Thought*. Garden City, NY: Garden City Press, 1954.

Xenophon. *Conversations of Socrates*, ed. Hugh Tredennick. New York: Penguin, 1990.

On the Internet

The Life of Socrates
www.2020site.org/socrates

The Last Days of Socrates, Philosophy Department, Clarke College (with Spanish translation)
socrates.clarke.edu/

Greek Philosophy
www.wsu.edu/~dee/GREECE/SOCRATES.htm

Index